UNDERSTANDING AND MANAGING YOUR EMOTIONS:

AN ESSENTIAL GUIDE TO ANGER MANAGEMENT

Carol Harrell

Table of Contents

CHAPTER 1

INTRODUCTION TO ANGER MANAGEMENT

Lizzy was an outgoing, passionate person who was quick to anger. She was always losing her temper and it was starting to affect her relationships with others. One day, she decided that she had to do something to control her anger.

She started by grabbing a copy of this book and learning how to take deep breaths and counting to ten when she felt her anger building. She also began to practice mindful meditation and visualization, picturing herself in a calm and peaceful place when she felt her anger rising.

By doing these things, she was able to learn how to control her anger better. She also started to express her feelings in healthier ways, such as talking to a trusted friend or writing in a journal.

With time and practice, Lizzy was able to manage her anger and build more positive relationships with the people around her. She had finally found a way to stay calm and peaceful, even in the most stressful of situations.

Anger management is a set of techniques and practices intended to help an individual recognize and cope with anger. It can help a person release pent-up emotions, learn better ways to express frustration, and develop healthier ways of communicating and resolving conflicts. Through anger management, individuals can learn how to identify and manage their triggers, take responsibility for their emotions, and learn how to better control their reactions to difficult situations. With a better understanding of how anger works and how to manage it, individuals can improve their relationships and overall well-being.

When learning about anger management, it is important to understand that anger is a normal emotion. It is a natural response to feeling threatened, frustrated, or overwhelmed. While it is important to recognize and accept anger, it is also important to learn how to express it in a healthy way. With the right tools and techniques, individuals can develop a better understanding of how to respond when they are feeling angry. By learning how to control their emotions, they can develop healthier ways of communicating and dealing with conflicts.

Ultimately, anger management can be a valuable tool for those who want to better understand and manage their emotions. With the right techniques and practices, individuals can gain a better understanding of how anger works and how to manage it in a constructive and healthy way.

CHAPTER 2

IDENTIFYING AND UNDERSTANDING YOUR ANGER I

IDENTIFYING YOUR ANGER

Anger is a natural emotion and it is important to identify and understand when it arises. It is an emotion that we experience in response to perceived threats or perceived injustices. It is an emotion that can be both positive and negative depending on the situation and how it is expressed.

Anger can be a sign of strength, as it can motivate us to take action when it is necessary. It can also be a sign of vulnerability, as it can be used to mask other emotions such as fear or hurt. It is important to identify and understand what is causing your anger so that it can be expressed in a constructive manner.

There are many different triggers that can cause anger. These can range from feeling powerless or not being able to get your needs met, to feeling neglected or unappreciated. It can also be triggered by feeling a lack of control over a situation or feeling overwhelmed.

IDENTIFYING YOUR ANGER TRIGGERS INCLUDE

1.Paying attention to your thoughts and feelings: You can recognize when you're feeling angry by paying attention to the thoughts and feelings that you are having. You can identify your anger triggers by noticing when you start to feel frustrated, irritated, or overwhelmed.

2. Taking time to reflect: Taking the time to reflect on your emotions and the situation that caused it can help you to identify what triggered your anger. You can think about what you were doing or saying, who you were talking to, or what you were feeling before the anger began.

3. Recognizing patterns: You can look for patterns in your behavior that might indicate you are about to become angry. **"Do I become angry when someone disagrees with me?" "Do I get angry when**

I'm feeling overwhelmed or stressed?". Identifying patterns can help you to anticipate your anger and work to prevent it.

4. **Paying attention to your body:** Paying attention to your body can also help you to identify your anger triggers. **"Am I feeling tense?" "Are my fists clenched?" "Is my heart racing?"**. Becoming aware of these physical signs can alert you to the fact that you're becoming angry and can help you to identify what triggered it.

5. **Talking to someone:** Talking to someone that you trust, such as a friend or family member, can also help you to identify your anger triggers. Explaining what you are

feeling and why can help you to gain clarity on what is causing your anger.

By taking the time to identify your anger triggers, you can work to prevent it from occurring in the future. This can help you to manage your anger in a healthier way and lead to better outcomes. It can be a powerful tool for personal growth and for developing healthy relationships.

UNDERSTANDING YOUR ANGER

Anger is a normal emotion that everyone experiences. It is important to understand why we feel angry and how to manage and express it in a healthy way.

Anger is a sign that something is wrong and needs to be addressed. It can arise from feeling frustrated, hurt, or powerless. It can also be a response to perceived injustice or mistreatment.

When we understand our anger, we can make better decisions about how to respond. We can identify triggers that set off our anger, and learn how to calm ourselves down before we lash out. We can also learn how to express our anger in a constructive way, such as setting healthy boundaries or communicating our feelings.

Understanding our anger can also help us see the root causes of our anger, such as past trauma or unresolved feelings. We can then work to resolve these issues in order to better manage our anger in the future and prevent it from causing harm.

CHAPTER 3

IDENTIFYING AND UNDERSTANDING YOUR ANGER II

TYPES OF ANGER

1. **Explosive Anger:** This type of anger is characterized by sudden, intense outbursts of rage. It is often the result of feeling overwhelmed by multiple stressors.

2. **Passive Aggressive Anger:** This type of anger is characterized by indirect expression of hostility. It can manifest as sarcasm, procrastination, or other forms of subtle hostility.

3. **Suppressed Anger:** This type of anger involves trying to hide or ignore feelings of anger, often to the point of self-harm. It can lead to feelings of depression and guilt.

4. **Judgmental Anger:** This type of anger involves making judgments about other people and their behavior. It can manifest as criticism or holding grudges.

5. **Chronic Anger:** This type of anger is long-term, persistent, and often difficult to manage. It can lead to a cycle of destructive behavior and poor decision making.

6. **Anxiety-Based Anger:** This type of anger is rooted in anxiety and fear. It is often

caused by feeling overwhelmed and can manifest as irritability.

7. Displaced Anger: This type of anger involves redirecting feelings of anger towards a person or object that is not the source of the anger.

8. Jealous Anger: This type of anger is caused by feelings of envy towards another person. It can lead to possessiveness or other destructive behavior.

9. Shame-Based Anger: This type of anger is caused by feelings of guilt or embarrassment. It may lead to aggressive behavior or self-sabotage.

SIGNS OF ANGER

1. **Verbal Aggression:** Verbal aggression is a sign of anger that involves threatening language, name-calling, sarcasm, or shouting.

2. **Physical Aggression:** Physical aggression is a sign of anger that involves hitting, pushing, or throwing objects.

3. **Facial Expressions:** Facial expressions can be a sign of anger, including clenched jaws, narrowed eyes, or frowning.

4. **Body Language:** Body language can also be a sign of anger, such as pointing fingers, crossing arms, or pacing.

5. **Irritability:** Irritability is another sign of anger, which can involve snapping at people or having a short temper.

6. **Avoidance:** Avoidance is a sign of anger in which the individual chooses to stay away from people or situations that trigger their anger.

7. **Substance Abuse:** Substance abuse can also be a sign of anger, as some people turn to drugs or alcohol to cope with their feelings of anger.

8. **Hostility:** Hostility is another sign of anger, which involves having a cynical or hostile outlook on life.

9. Anxiety: Anxiety can be a sign of anger, as feeling angry can lead to feelings of anxiety and stress.

10. Depression: Depression can also be a sign of anger, as feeling angry can lead to difficulty sleeping, loss of appetite, and feelings of sadness and hopelessness.

11. Health Complications: Health complications can also be a sign of anger, as chronic anger can lead to high blood pressure, headaches, and other physical health problems.

12. Self-Harm: Self-harm is another sign of anger, as some people turn to self-harm in order to cope with their feelings of anger.

13. **Suicidal Thoughts**: Suicidal thoughts can also be a sign of anger, as feeling angry can lead to thoughts of suicide.

14. **Outbursts:** Outbursts are another sign of anger, as some people have difficulty controlling their anger and can become explosive.

15. **Resentment:** Resentment is another sign of anger, as feeling angry can lead to feelings of resentment toward another person or toward a situation.

16. **Withdrawal:** Withdrawal is also a sign of anger, as some people choose to isolate themselves when they are feeling angry.

17. Self-Destructive Behavior: Self-destructive behavior is another sign of anger, as some people will engage in risky or harmful behaviors in order to cope with their feelings of anger.

18. Social Isolation: Social isolation is another sign of anger, as some people choose to avoid social situations when they are feeling angry.

19. Excessive Rumination: Excessive rumination is another sign of anger, as some people can become stuck in a cycle of ruminating on their anger and the source of their anger.

20. Emotional Outbursts: Emotional outbursts are another sign of anger, as some people may have difficulty controlling their emotions when they are feeling angry.

21. Uncontrolled Thoughts: Uncontrolled thoughts are another sign of anger, as feeling angry can lead to racing thoughts and difficulty concentrating.

22. Apathy: Apathy is another sign of anger, as some people may experience a lack of emotion when they are feeling angry.

23. Lashing Out: Lashing out is another sign of anger, as some people may have difficulty controlling their anger and may take it out on others.

24. Feeling Detached: Feeling detached is another sign of anger, as some people may feel disconnected from themselves and their emotions when they are feeling angry.

25. Repressed Anger: Repressed anger is another sign of anger, as some people may be unable to express their anger in a healthy way.

26. Paranoia: Paranoia is another sign of anger, as feeling angry can lead to irrational thoughts and fear of others.

27. Blaming Others: Blaming others is another sign of anger, as some people may be unable to take responsibility for their feelings and instead blame others for their anger.

28. Unhealthy Coping Strategies: Unhealthy coping strategies can also be a sign of anger, as some people may turn to unhealthy behaviors such as overeating or substance use in order to cope with their anger.

29. Impatience: Impatience is another sign of anger, as some people may become frustrated easily when they are feeling angry.

30. Low Self-Esteem: Low self-esteem can also be a sign of anger, as feeling angry can lead to negative self-talk and a lack of self-confidence.

31. Hypervigilance: Hypervigilance is another sign of anger, as some people may become overly vigilant and suspicious when they are feeling angry.

32. Self-Sabotage: Self-sabotage is another sign of anger, as some people may act in ways that are counterproductive to their goals or desires when they are feeling angry.

33. Denial: Denial is another sign of anger, as some people may not want to acknowledge their feelings of anger.

34. Overreacting: Overreacting is another sign of anger, as some people may become overly emotional or take things too seriously when they are feeling angry.

35. Uncontrollable Rage: Uncontrollable rage is another sign of anger, as some people may become overwhelmed by their anger and unable to control their behavior.

CAUSES OF ANGER

The causes of anger include:

1. **Frustration:** Frustration occurs when expectations or desires are not met. This can lead to feelings of anger and resentment.

2. **Miscommunication:** Miscommunication, such as not understanding another's point of view, can lead to feelings of anger.

3. **Unfair Treatment:** Perceived injustice or unfair treatment can lead to feelings of anger and resentment.

4. **Inadequacy:** Feelings of inadequacy or inferiority can lead to feelings of anger.

5. **Stress:** Stressful situations can lead to feelings of anger.

6. **Threats:** Perceived threats to one's safety or well-being can lead to feelings of anger.

7. **Loss:** Feelings of loss or grief can lead to anger.

8. **Fear:** Fear can lead to feelings of anger and aggression.

9. **Embarrassment:** Embarrassment or humiliation can lead to feelings of anger.

10. **Jealousy:** Jealousy can lead to feelings of anger, especially when someone feels they are being unfairly treated or overlooked.

11. Powerlessness: A feeling of powerlessness or helplessness can lead to feelings of anger.

12. Revenge: Feelings of revenge can lead to feelings of anger.

13. Defensiveness: Feelings of defensiveness can lead to feelings of anger.

14. Injustice: Perceived injustice can lead to feelings of anger.

15. Unmet needs: Unmet needs or expectations can lead to feelings of anger.

16. Conflict: Conflict between two people or groups can lead to feelings of anger and hostility.

17. Physical pain: Physical pain or discomfort can lead to feelings of anger.

18. Drug or alcohol abuse: Substance abuse can lead to feelings of anger.

19. Cultural differences: Different cultural interpretations and beliefs can lead to feelings of anger.

20. Impulsivity: Impulsive or reckless behavior can lead to feelings of anger.

21. Mental health issues: Mental health issues, such as depression or anxiety, can lead to feelings of anger.

22. Rejection: People may become angry when they feel that they have been rejected or ignored.

23. Guilt: People may get angry when they feel guilty or ashamed of something they have done.

24. Exhaustion: People may become angry when they are exhausted and not able to cope with their emotions.

25. Disagreement: People may become angry when they disagree with someone else's opinion or point of view.

26. Loneliness: People may become angry when they feel isolated or neglected.

27. Hormonal changes: Hormonal changes, such as those experienced during puberty, menopause, or pregnancy, can lead to increased irritability and anger.

28. Genetics: Research suggests that there may be a genetic component to anger and aggression.

29. Learned behavior: People may have learned to express their anger in unhealthy ways, such as shouting and violence, from their parents or other authority figures.

30. Environmental factors: People who live in high-stress environments, such as poverty or conflict areas, may be more prone to anger.

31. Lack of problem-solving skills: When people are unable to find solutions to their problems, they may become frustrated and angry.

32. Lack of control: People may become angry when they feel like they have no control over a situation.

33. Unfulfilled expectations: People may become angry when they feel like their expectations have not been met.

34. Lack of assertiveness: People who do not express their needs and feelings in a constructive way may become angry.

35. Unchecked emotions: If people are unable to manage their emotions, it can lead to anger.

36. Blaming: When people blame others for their problems, it can lead to feelings of anger and resentment.

37. Sense of superiority: People may become angry when they feel like they are better than someone else.

38. Low self-esteem: People may become angry when they feel insecure or inadequate.

39. Unreasonable expectations: When people set unrealistic expectations for themselves or others, it can lead to anger.

39. Inability to cope: People may become angry when they are unable to cope with a situation.

40. **Prejudice:** People may become angry when they feel like they are the victims of prejudice or discrimination.

41. **Chronic Illness:** People with chronic illnesses may become angry more easily, as they may feel that their condition is limiting their ability to live a normal life.

42. **Cognitive Dysfunction:** Cognitive dysfunction or brain injuries can lead to difficulty managing emotions, which can lead to feelings of anger.

43. **Social Rejection:** Social rejection can lead to feelings of anger and aggression.

44. Financial Problems: Financial problems can lead to feelings of anger and frustration.

45. Unfair Criticism: Unfair criticism can lead to feelings of anger and resentment.

46. Lack of Appreciation: When someone feels that their efforts are not appreciated, it can lead to feelings of anger.

EFFECTS OF ANGER

Anger is a strong emotion that can have both physical and psychological effects on a person.

Physical effects of anger include:

1. **Increased heart rate:** Anger can cause an increase in heart rate, as the body prepares itself to respond to a perceived threat.

2. **Shallow breathing:** When a person is angry, their breathing may become shallow and rapid, as the body attempts to take in more oxygen in order to fuel the fight-or-flight response.

3. **Increased blood pressure:** Anger can cause an increase in blood pressure, as the body responds to the stress of the situation.

4. **Muscle tension**: A person may experience increased muscle tension when they are angry, as the body prepares itself for action.

5. **Sweating**: Sweating is a common physical response to anger, as the body attempts to cool itself down.

6. **Flushed skin**: Anger can cause a person's skin to become flushed, as blood rushes to the skin in order to help regulate body temperature.

7. **Clenched fists**: Clenching one's fists is a common physical response to anger, as the body attempts to prepare itself for action.

8. Gritting teeth: Gritting one's teeth is another common physical response to anger, as the body attempts to prepare itself for action.

9. Headache: Anger can cause a person to experience a headache, as the body responds to the stress of the situation.

10. Stomachache: Anger can cause a person to experience a stomachache, as the body responds to the stress of the situation.

11. Nausea: Nausea is a common physical response to anger, as the body attempts to rid itself of whatever is causing the anger.

12. **Insomnia:** Anger can cause a person to have difficulty falling asleep, as the body is still in fight-or-flight mode.

13. **Shaking:** Shaking is a common physical response to anger, as the body attempts to rid itself of built-up tension.

14. **Fatigue:** Anger can cause a person to become fatigued, as the body expends energy in an attempt to cope with the stress.

15. **Aggression:** Anger can lead to aggressive behavior, as the body attempts to protect itself from the perceived threat.

Psychologically, anger can cause:

1. Increased Blood Pressure/Heart Rate: Anger can cause a sudden increase in blood pressure and heart rate, which can have a damaging effect on the heart and circulatory system over time.

2. Stress: Anger can be a source of immense stress, which can lead to physical and emotional symptoms such as headaches, insomnia, anxiety, and depression.

3. Aggression: Anger can cause aggressive behavior, including property damage, verbal abuse, and physical violence.

4. **Poor Judgment:** Anger can lead to impulsive decisions and thought processes that can have a damaging effect on relationships, careers, and other areas of life.

5. **Isolation:** Anger can lead to social isolation, as people may avoid those who are angry out of fear or discomfort.

6. **Health Problems:** Anger can lead to a range of physical health problems, such as high blood pressure, heart disease, and digestive issues.

7. **Guilt:** Anger can lead to feelings of guilt, as people may regret their actions or words after the fact.

8. Low Self-Esteem: Anger can lead to low self-esteem, as people may feel embarrassed or ashamed of their behavior.

9. Self-Destructive Behavior: Anger can lead to self-destructive behavior, such as substance abuse, overeating, or reckless behavior.

10. Loss of Control: Anger can lead to a feeling of being out of control, which can be frightening and overwhelming.

11. Difficulty Concentrating: Anger can lead to difficulty concentrating, which can interfere with work, school, and other areas of life.

12. **Emotional Paralysis:** Anger can lead to an inability to think clearly, process emotions, or take action.

13. **Unhappiness:** Anger can lead to long-term unhappiness and dissatisfaction, as people may become stuck in a cycle of anger and frustration.

14. **Burnout:** Anger can lead to burnout, as people may become exhausted from constantly dealing with difficult emotions.

15. **Health Complications:** Anger can lead to health complications, such as headaches, stomach upset, and high blood pressure.

Long-term, anger can also cause strained relationships, low self-esteem, and problems at work or school.

If left unchecked, anger can also lead to destructive behaviors such as substance abuse or violent outbursts. It is important to recognize the signs of anger and learn how to manage it effectively.

CHAPTER 4

STRATEGIES FOR MANAGING ANGER

These can be grouped under:

1. Cognitive strategies
2. Behavioral strategies
3. Relaxation strategies

COGNITIVE STRATEGIES FOR MANAGING ANGER

1.Reframing: This is a cognitive strategy that involves looking at a situation from a different perspective. It involves identifying underlying assumptions, beliefs, and interpretations that may be contributing to feelings of anger. This strategy can help individuals to see the situation from a different angle and see alternative solutions to their problem.

2. Cognitive Appraisal: This cognitive strategy involves evaluating the situation objectively and rationally to determine the extent of the problem and the potential solutions available. This can help individuals to gain a better understanding of the situation and identify possible alternatives to responding with anger.

3. Cognitive Restructuring: This is a cognitive strategy that involves challenging and replacing negative thoughts and beliefs with more balanced and rational ones. It can help individuals to identify and modify their thinking patterns and beliefs in a more constructive manner.

4. Self-Talk: This cognitive strategy involves individuals talking to themselves in a positive and supportive manner. It can help to provide a sense of perspective and reduce feelings of anger.

5. Relaxation Techniques: This is a cognitive strategy that involves using techniques such as deep breathing and progressive muscle relaxation to help individuals to calm down and reduce feelings of anger.

6. Distraction: This is a cognitive strategy that involves engaging in activities such as reading, listening to music, or taking a walk to help individuals to take their mind off the situation and focus on something else. This can help to reduce feelings of anger and create a sense of calm.

7. Problem-Solving: This cognitive strategy involves identifying the problem and then brainstorming potential solutions. This can help individuals to come up with constructive solutions to their problems and reduce feelings of anger.

8. Assertiveness: This cognitive strategy involves expressing feelings and opinions in an assertive and respectful manner. This can help to reduce feelings of anger and create a more positive outcome.

These are some of the cognitive strategies that can be used to help manage anger. It is important to remember that different strategies may work better for different individuals, so it is important to experiment and find what works best for you.

BEHAVIORAL STRATEGIES FOR MANAGING ANGER

1. Express Feelings Appropriately: Allow yourself to express your feelings of anger in a productive and non-threatening manner. This might include talking to someone you trust, writing in a journal, or using deep breathing and relaxation exercises to help manage your emotions.

2. Take a Time-Out: Taking a break from the situation can be a great way to help you calm down and regain control. A few minutes away from the situation can give you space to assess the situation and gain perspective.

3. Problem-Solve: Try to identify the source of your anger and then brainstorm solutions. Whether it's an issue with another person or an ongoing problem in your life, understanding the issue and working towards a solution can help to reduce your anger.

4. Use Humor: Using humor can be a great way to help you manage your anger. It can help to lighten the mood and provide a distraction from the situation at hand.

5. Practice Relaxation Techniques: Relaxation techniques such as deep breathing, visualization, and meditation can help to reduce stress and provide a sense of calm and relaxation.

6. Exercise: Exercise can be a great way to help manage anger. It can help to release endorphins, reduce stress, and provide a distraction from the situation causing your anger.

7. Talk to Someone: Talking to someone you trust about your feelings can be a great way to help you manage your anger. Having someone listen to your concerns and provide support can help to reduce your anger and provide you with a sense of relief.

8. Identify Triggers: Identifying what triggers your anger can be a great way to help you manage it. Understanding what causes your anger can help you to be proactive in avoiding situations and people that trigger your emotions.

9. Reframe Your Thoughts: Reframing your thoughts can help to reduce your anger. Instead of letting negative thoughts consume you, try to think of the situation in a more positive light. This can help to reduce your anger and provide you with a sense of optimism.

10. Avoid Unhelpful Behaviors: Avoiding unhelpful behaviors, such as yelling and arguing, can help to reduce your anger. Taking a step back and focusing on positive behaviors can help to reduce your anger and provide you with a sense of control.

11. Practice Mindfulness: Practicing mindfulness can help to reduce your anger by teaching you to become aware of your thoughts and feelings and to accept them without judgment. This can help to reduce your anger and provide you with a sense of peace and clarity.

12. Seek Professional Help: If you find that your anger is unmanageable, seeking professional help can be a great way to help you learn how to manage your emotions. A therapist can help you to gain insight into your emotions and provide you with strategies to manage your anger.

These are some of the most common behavioral strategies for managing anger. With practice and dedication, these strategies can help you to better manage your emotions and provide you with a sense of control and calm.

RELAXATION STRATEGIES FOR MANAGING ANGER

1. Count to 10: This relaxation strategy encourages the person to take a few moments to pause and take deep breaths before responding to a situation. Counting to 10 can help to give the person time to think about how to react calmly, rather than in an angry way.

2. Take a Time-Out: Taking a short break from a situation can help to give the person time to cool down and gain perspective. This can involve either stepping away from the situation or simply taking a few moments to sit quietly and think.

3. Breathe Deeply: Deep breathing is a great way to relax and calm down. Taking slow, deep breaths can help to reduce tension and stress, as well as allow the person to gain control over their emotions.

4. Exercise: Physical activity is a great way to release pent-up energy and reduce stress. Exercise can help to clear the mind and refocus the person's thoughts away from anger.

5. Think Positively: Thinking positively can help to reduce anger and stress. Taking a few moments to think about the positive aspects of a situation can help to put it into perspective and give the person a more positive outlook.

6. Talk it Out: Talking to someone can help to release built up emotions and gain perspective on the situation. Talking to a friend, family member or trusted professional can help to relieve tension and gain insight into the situation.

7. Use Humor: Humor can be a great tool for managing anger. Taking a few moments to laugh can help to relieve stress and gain perspective.

8. Write it Down: Writing down thoughts and feelings can help to release built up emotions and gain clarity on the situation. Writing can also help to gain insight into why the person is feeling angry and how to manage it in the future.

9. Visualize: Visualization is a great relaxation technique that can help to gain perspective on a situation. Visualizing a peaceful scene or a positive outcome can help to reduce stress and gain control over the emotions.

10. Listen to Music: Music can be a great way to relax and gain perspective. Taking a few moments to listen to calming music can help to reduce stress and gain clarity on the situation.

11. Practice Mindfulness: Mindfulness is a great way to gain control over emotions and gain perspective on a situation. Taking a few moments to focus on the present moment can help to reduce stress and focus the mind away from anger.

12. Talk to Yourself: Taking a few moments to talk to yourself can help to gain control over emotions. Talking to yourself in a positive and calming way can help to reduce stress and gain clarity on the situation.

13. Practice Self Care: Taking time to practice self-care can help to reduce stress and gain control over emotions. Self-care can be anything from taking a hot bath to going on a walk.

14. Use Aromatherapy: Aromatherapy can be a great way to relax and reduce stress. Taking a few moments to smell a soothing scent such as lavender can help to reduce tension and gain clarity on the situation.

15. Meditate: Meditation is a great way to relax and gain control over emotions. Taking a few moments to meditate can help to reduce stress and gain clarity on the situation.

16. Do Something Creative: Doing something creative can be a great way to reduce stress and gain control over emotions. Taking a few moments to draw, paint, write, or do something else creative can help to reduce tension and gain perspective.

17. Play with a Pet: Spending time with a pet can be a great way to reduce stress and gain control over emotions. Taking a few moments to play with a pet can help to reduce tension and gain perspective.

18. Take a Hot Shower: Taking a hot shower can be a great way to relax and reduce stress. Taking a few moments to relax in a hot shower can help to reduce tension and gain clarity on the situation.

19. Practice Yoga: Practicing yoga can be a great way to reduce stress and gain control over emotions. Taking a few moments to practice yoga can help to reduce tension and gain perspective.

20. Create a List: Creating a list of things that make you happy can help to reduce stress and gain control over emotions. Taking a few moments to make a list can help to reduce tension and gain clarity on the situation.

21. Use Guided Imagery: Guided imagery is a great way to relax and gain control over emotions. Taking a few moments to focus on a guided imagery exercise can help to reduce tension and gain perspective.

22. Take a Nap: Taking a nap can be a great way to relax and reduce stress. Taking a few moments to rest can help to reduce tension and gain clarity on the situation.

23. Stretch: Stretching can be a great way to reduce stress and gain control over emotions. Taking a few moments to stretch can help to reduce tension and gain perspective.

24. Listen to Nature Sounds: Listening to nature sounds can be a great way to relax and reduce stress. Taking a few moments to listen to calming nature sounds can help to reduce tension and gain clarity on the situation.

25. Journal: Keeping a journal can be a great way to reduce stress and gain control over emotions. Taking a few moments to write down thoughts and feelings can help to reduce tension and gain perspective.

26. Practice Relaxation Techniques:

Relaxation techniques such as progressive muscle relaxation and autogenic training can be a great way to reduce stress and gain control over emotions. Taking a few moments to practice these techniques can help to reduce tension and gain clarity on the situation.

CHAPTER 5

LEARNING TO COMMUNICATE EFFECTIVELY

Tips on learning to communicate effectively when angry

1. Take a Time Out: When feeling overwhelmed by anger, it is important to take a step back and take a time out. Taking a moment to pause and reset can help to regain composure and calm down.

2. Express Feelings: When communicating effectively when angry, it is important to express feelings in a clear and appropriate way. Instead of lashing out, try to express feelings in a constructive manner.

3. Listen: In order to communicate effectively when angry, it is important to listen to the other person's perspective. Try to understand where the other person is coming from and focus on finding a resolution.

4. Be Respectful: It is important to remember to be respectful when communicating your feelings. Even when feeling angry, try to remain respectful of the other person and use language that is not inflammatory.

5. Focus on Solutions: Instead of getting caught up in the emotions of the moment, focus on finding solutions to the problem at hand. This can help to move the conversation away from arguing and towards a constructive solution.

6. Avoid Assumptions: When communicating effectively when angry, it is important to avoid making assumptions. Instead of jumping to conclusions, try to get clarification and ensure that everyone is on the same page.

7. Take Responsibility: Finally, it is important to take responsibility for one's own actions and words. Acknowledge when one may have been wrong and take ownership of mistakes. This can help to foster healthier communication.

By following these tips, it is possible to communicate effectively even when feeling angry. Taking a moment to pause, expressing feelings in a constructive manner, listening to the other person, being respectful, and focusing on solutions can help to promote effective communication.

CHAPTER 6

WORKING WITH OTHERS TO MANAGE ANGER

The following are steps to work with others to manage anger

1. Establish Ground Rules: Work with the other person to clarify expectations and establish ground rules for how to handle anger. Discuss topics such as language, volume, time limits, and strategies for calming down.

2. Communicate Openly: When working with others, it's important to talk openly and honestly about your feelings of anger.

Don't be afraid to express your concerns in a respectful way and make sure you are heard.

3. Listen Carefully: Listening to the other person's perspective can help you better understand their feelings and the situation. This can help you manage your own anger and determine a constructive way forward.

4. Take a Time Out: If the situation becomes too heated, take a break. This will give you a chance to cool down and think through your feelings.

5. Practice Self-Control: Take deep breaths and practice staying grounded.

This can help you stay in control and make decisions more calmly.

6. Identify the Problem: Work with the other person to identify the root cause of their anger.

7. Consider Solutions: Consider any potential solutions or compromises to the issue at hand. Make sure to be respectful and open to the other person's point of view.

8. Acknowledge Feelings: Acknowledge the other person's feelings and validate them.

9. Make a Plan: Develop a plan of action that both parties can agree on and commit to following.

10. Follow Through: Make sure that both parties follow through on the plan.

11. Reflect: Reflect on what happened and how it could have been managed better.

12. Seek Outside Help: If the situation persists, consider seeking professional help or guidance. This can help you build effective strategies for managing anger and working through the issue.

13. Move Forward: Move forward with a new understanding and acceptance of the situation.

These steps can help you work with others to manage anger in a constructive and healthy way.

CHAPTER 7

PRACTICING MINDFULNESS AND SELF-CARE

When you feel angry, it can be difficult to stay mindful and take care of yourself. However, it is important to practice mindfulness and self-care when angry in order to avoid further escalation of your emotions.

Below are the steps in practicing mindfulness and self-care when angry:

1.Take a few deep breaths: Taking a few deep breaths can help to calm down the body and mind in order to gain clarity and perspective on the situation. It can also help to release tension and reduce stress.

2. Identify your triggers: Pay attention to your body and mind to identify the triggers that are causing your anger. This will help you to be aware of what is causing your emotions and how you can better manage them.

3. Practice self-compassion: When angry, it is important to practice self-compassion and talk to yourself in a kind and understanding way. This will help to reduce the intensity of your emotions and provide a sense of understanding and acceptance.

4. Take a break: It is important to step away from the situation and take a break. This can be a physical break where you leave the environment, or a mental break where you focus on something else such as listening to music or reading a book.

5. Find an outlet: Find an outlet for your anger such as exercising, writing, or talking to a friend. This can help to release the energy associated with the emotion and provide an opportunity to process your feelings.

6. Reflect: Once you have calmed down, take the time to reflect on the situation and determine if there are any lessons to be learned. This will help you to better manage your emotions in the future.

7. Practice self-care: Lastly, it is important to practice self-care and engage in activities that bring you joy and peace. This can help to rebuild and restore your sense of inner balance.

By following these steps, you can practice mindfulness and self-care when angry, allowing you to better manage your emotions and reduce the intensity of your anger.

Take the time to find what works best for you and remember that you are in control of your emotions.

CHAPTER 8

Moving Forward with Healthy Anger Management

1. **Acknowledge your anger:** Take some time to reflect on why you are feeling angry. Identify the source of your anger and try to understand it.

2. **Find healthy outlets for your anger:** Take up a physical activity or hobby to help you channel your anger into something productive.

3. **Practice relaxation techniques:** Take some deep breaths or practice yoga and

meditation to help you relax and reduce your stress levels.

4. **Avoid problem triggers:** Identify what triggers your anger and try to avoid them or find healthier ways to cope with them.

5. **Manage your thoughts:** When you feel anger rising, take a step back and remind yourself of positive thoughts.

6. **Seek professional help:** If you are still struggling to manage your anger, consider speaking to a mental health professional for advice and guidance.

7. **Take care of yourself:** Be sure you have enough sleep, exercise and consume a

balanced diet. These will help you stay healthy and better equipped to manage your anger.

8. Make time for yourself: Take some time out to relax and enjoy activities that make you feel good.

SEEKING SUPPORT WHEN ANGRY

When feeling angry, it can be beneficial to seek support from a trusted friend, family member, or therapist. This can help to process the emotions in a healthy way, and provide an outlet for releasing tension. It can also help to talk through potential solutions or strategies to resolve the issue.

It can be helpful to practice relaxation techniques such as deep breathing, progressive muscle relaxation, mindfulness, or other coping mechanisms to help manage the anger. Seeking support during times of anger can help to provide perspective and insight, which can be beneficial in finding a resolution.

CONCLUSION

Anger management is an important skill that everyone should learn. It helps us to regulate our emotions in a constructive way, express our feelings in a healthy manner, and find better solutions to difficult situations. It also teaches us how to be more mindful and aware of ourselves and our emotions. With regular practice, we can develop the capacity to take control of our anger and use it to create positive change in our lives.

There is no one-size-fits-all solution to dealing with anger, but there are many techniques that can help us better manage our emotions. By understanding our triggers, identifying our feelings, and learning to be mindful of our reactions, we can use anger in a way that leads to positive outcomes. With patience and practice, we can learn to handle our anger in a productive and healthy way.

In conclusion, anger is a normal emotion, but when it is not managed in a healthy manner, it can lead to negative consequences. With the right tools and techniques, we can better understand and control our anger and use it as a catalyst for positive change in our lives.

www.ingramcontent.com/pod-product-compliance
Lightning Source LLC
LaVergne TN
LVHW052052160826
845678LV00015B/3186